The Rising Hope

ENCOURAGEMENT *for* YOUR HEART

Charles R. Swindoll

THOMAS NELSON
Since 1798

NASHVILLE   DALLAS   MEXICO CITY   RIO DE JANEIRO   BEIJING

The Rising Hope

© 2009 by Charles R. Swindoll

All rights reserved. No portion of this book may be reproduced, stored in a retrieval system, or transmitted in any form or by any means—electronic, mechanical, photocopy, recording, scanning, or other—except for brief quotations in critical reviews or articles, without the prior written permission of the publisher.

Published in Nashville, Tennessee. Thomas Nelson is a registered trademark of Thomas Nelson, Inc.

Thomas Nelson, Inc. titles may be purchased in bulk for educational, business, fundraising, or sales promotional use. For information, please e-mail SpecialMarkets@ThomasNelson.com.

Portions of this book were adapted from *Simple Faith* and *Laugh Again* by Charles R. Swindoll © 2008. Used by permission.

Unless otherwise marked, Scripture quotations are taken from New American Standard Bible, © 1960, 1977, 1995 by the Lockman Foundation. Used by permission.

Scripture quotations marked NKJV are taken from The New King James Version. © 1982 by Thomas Nelson, Inc. Used by permission. All rights reserved.

Scripture quotations marked NCV are taken from the New Century Version®. © 2005 by Thomas Nelson, Inc. Used by permission. All rights reserved.

Scripture quotations marked NLT are taken from the *Holy Bible*, New Living Translation. © 1996, 2004. Used by permission of Tyndale House Publishers, Inc., Wheaton, Illinois 60189. All rights reserved.

Scripture quotations marked NET are taken from The NET Bible, New English Translation (NET). © 1996–2007 by Biblical Studies Press, L.L.C., www.bible.org. All rights reserved.

Library of Congress Cataloging-in-Publication Data

Swindoll, Charles R.
    The rising hope : encouragement for your heart / Charles R. Swindoll.
        p. cm.
    ISBN 978-1-4002-0248-5
    1. Hope—Religious aspects—Christianity. I. Title.
BV4638.S95 2009
234'.25—dc22   2008044836

Printed in the United States of America

08 09 10 11 12 QW 9 8 7 6 5 4 3 2 1

The Rising Hope

ENCOURAGEMENT *for* YOUR HEART

Listen to the news media on any given day, and you probably wonder, *Is there any hope left?* Soaring energy prices, weather-related catastrophes, economic instability, military conflict, crime, layoffs, suicides—and on and on. Even closer to home, perhaps you struggle with hopelessness about your marriage, children, job, friendships, or other things you hold dear.

We all need hope! When enduring life's most difficult times, we need to believe that a positive outcome is possible.

- When we are trapped in a tunnel of misery, hope points to the light at the end.

- When we are overworked and exhausted, hope gives us fresh energy.

- When we are discouraged, hope lifts our spirits.

- When we are tempted to quit, hope keeps us going.

- When we lose our way and confusion blurs the destination, hope dulls the edge of panic.

- When we fear the worst, hope reminds us that God is still in control.

- When we must endure the consequences of God's decisions, hope fuels our recovery.

- When we find ourselves unemployed, hope tells us we still have a future.

- When we are forced to sit back and wait, hope gives us the patience to trust.

- When we feel rejected and abandoned, hope reminds us we're not alone.

- When we say our final farewell to someone we love, hope of life beyond the grave gets us through our grief.

Hope isn't optional. It's essential to our survival. Hope is as important to us as water is to a fish, as vital as electricity is to a light bulb, as essential as air is to a jumbo jet. Hope is basic to life. We cannot stay on the road to our dreams without it, at least not very far. Many have tried—none successfully. Take away our hope, and our existence is reduced to depression and despair.

When life hurts and dreams fade, nothing helps like hope.

But where does hope come from? Is it something that we can cultivate within ourselves? Does positive thinking hold the key? *To what do you look for hope?*

Does Success Give Us Hope?

Fortune. Fame. Power. Pleasure. The messages bombard us from every direction. We devour books, CDs, websites, and seminars on everything from dressing for success to investing for success. But something very significant is absent in the pursuit of these things—a *vertical* dimension. In the pursuit of self-focused success—*our* goals, *our* plans, *our* projects, *our* accomplishments—there's not a hint of God's will or what pleases Him. And nothing in that horizontal list guarantees satisfaction or brings relief deep within the heart.

The world's strategy for success is simple: work hard, get ahead, and then climb higher—even if you have to step on the next guy to promote yourself. The goal is to make it to the top. It doesn't matter who you push aside along the way, and it doesn't matter who you leave behind, even if it's your family or your friends or your integrity. To succeed, you have to fight your way up . . . and never stop climbing.

Interestingly, very few of today's success gurus address what most people really want in life—contentment, fulfillment, satisfaction, and hope of a better tomorrow. Rarely, if ever, are we coached to set boundaries or encouraged to say, "Enough is enough." So we work harder and harder to make more and more, yet we enjoy all of it less and less.

Are you caught up in the success syndrome? Are you convinced that the world's formula is the best? Do you find yourself manipulating people and pulling strings to get ahead? No wonder you feel dissatisfied! That type of success *never* satisfies. Only God-directed success brings lasting contentment, fulfillment, satisfaction, and the hope you are longing for.

Is There Hope Today?

Today, there are many people inviting you to believe whatever you want to believe and do whatever you want to do. Yet that perspective does not lead to lasting peace. Nor does it offer genuine hope. Hope must have a firm foundation built upon truth.

Undoubtedly you have heard about many different religions in the world. All of them claim to offer hope, but only one offers credible proof to support its promises. There is only one faith in which people accurately foretold specific details about events that occurred hundreds of years later. Furthermore, there were many eyewitnesses to these anticipated events as they unfolded.

Let me share with you something that was foretold seven hundred years before it happened. In Isaiah 53:8–11, the writer penned these words about the coming Messiah:

Men took him away roughly and
    unfairly.
He died without children to continue
    his family.
He was put to death;
    he was punished for the sins of my
    people.
He was buried with wicked men,
    and he died with the rich.
He had done nothing wrong,
    and he had never lied.
But it was the Lord who decided
    to crush him and make him suffer.

The LORD made his life a penalty
     offering,
          but he will still see his descendants
          and live a long life.
He will complete the things the LORD
     wants him to do.
"After his soul suffers many things,
     he will see life and be satisfied.
My good servant will make many
     people right with God; he will carry
     away their sins. (NCV)

Seven hundred years later, what had
been foretold in the Old Testament book
of Isaiah came true and is described by an
eyewitness named Matthew:

Jesus was beaten with whips and handed
over to the soldiers to be crucified . . .

. . . At noon the whole country became dark, and the darkness lasted for three hours. About three o'clock Jesus cried out in a loud voice, "Eli, Eli, lama sabachthani?" This means, "My God, my God, why have you abandoned me?" . . . And Jesus cried out again with a loud voice, and yielded up His spirit. (Matthew 27:26, 45–46 NCV; 27:50 NASB)

When Jesus died just as the prophet Isaiah described beforehand, it would seem all hope was lost. But wait . . . the Isaiah passage above says, "He will see life and be satisfied." The prophet said that Jesus will "make many people right with God," and He will "carry away their sins" (vv. 11–12).

Not only was Jesus' death foretold seven hundred years before it occurred, His resurrection was predicted as well. In the gospel of Matthew, we read several different eyewitness accounts. Here's the first one:

The day after the Sabbath day was the first day of the week. At dawn on the first day, Mary Magdalene and another woman named Mary went to look at the tomb.

At that time there was a strong earthquake. An angel of the Lord came down from heaven, went to the tomb, and rolled the stone away from the entrance. Then he sat on the stone. He was shining as bright as lightning, and his clothes were white as snow. The soldiers guarding the tomb shook with fear because of the angel, and they became like dead men.

The angel said to the women, "Don't be afraid. I know that you are looking for Jesus, who has been crucified. He is not here. He has risen from the dead as he said he would. Come and see the place where his body was. And go quickly and tell his followers, 'Jesus has risen from the dead. He is going into Galilee ahead of you, and you will see him there.'" Then the angel said, "Now I have told you."

The women left the tomb quickly. They were afraid, but they were also very happy. They ran to tell Jesus' followers what had happened. Suddenly, Jesus met them and said, "Greetings." The women came up to him, took hold of his feet, and worshiped him. Then Jesus said to them, "Don't be afraid." (Matthew 28:1–10 NCV)

Here are two of the most important revelations you have ever encountered: (1) Jesus conquered death, and (2) Jesus said, "Don't be afraid."

Because Jesus is the Rising Hope for all of us, we never have to fear or live in despair!

Our enemies—Satan, sin, and the corrupt world system—want nothing more than to rob us of hope. If they can succeed in doing that, our effectiveness as witnesses will fade, and our earthly existence will be tragically cut short. Fortunately, God has not left us alone. His Holy Spirit lives within us to provide what we lack.

He will give us wisdom when we are foolish. He will give us peace when we doubt. He will give us assurance when we fail. And He will give us hope when Satan accuses, sin condemns, and the world causes suffering.

But I'm getting ahead of myself. The Holy Spirit is only promised to those who have a relationship with Jesus Christ. And a life without Christ is a life without hope.

Tragically, many people endure the inevitable difficulties of life without Jesus Christ. Without Christ for comfort, they spend sleepless nights in the hospital facing the likelihood of death. Without Christ for wisdom, they struggle to save a wayward teenager from self-destruction. Alone, they endure the awful words from a mate: "I don't love you anymore. I'm leaving." In sorrow, they lay their loved one in the grave with no promise of a peaceful eternity. And they go through it all without hope.

A Living Hope on Solid Foundation

> Blessed be the God and Father of our Lord Jesus Christ, who according to His abundant mercy has begotten us again to a living hope through the resurrection of Jesus Christ from the dead. (1 Peter 1:3)

Jesus was a master storyteller. He especially loved telling parables. Interesting word, *parable*—it means, literally, "to cast alongside." In other words, a parable is a story in which a familiar situation is cast alongside the unfamiliar for the purpose of illustration—making the unfamiliar clear and easy to grasp.

In the gospel of Matthew, Jesus tells this parable:

Therefore everyone who hears these words of Mine and acts on them, may be compared to a wise man who built his house on the rock. And the rain fell, and the floods came, and the winds blew and slammed against that house; and yet it did not fall, for it had been founded on the rock. Everyone who hears these words of Mine and does not act on them, will be like a foolish man who built his house on the sand. The rain fell, and the floods came, and the winds blew and slammed against that house; and it fell— and great was its fall. (7:24–27)

The main characters in this parable are two builders constructing two houses in two different locations. Of course, Jesus was not talking about building literal houses on literal rock and literal sand; He was talking about building lives—establishing values and determining priorities on contrasting philosophies or lifestyles.

Each house suffered a storm. Neither was able to escape it or ignore it. Both experienced the downpour. Both saw the flood waters rise and felt the sting of gale-force winds. Such storms are inevitable. Clearly Jesus was not telling us to find a safe, comfortable setting. On the contrary, His story forces us to face reality: life is difficult . . . storms are inevitable . . . pain and discomfort happen. There is no escaping life's calamities.

The two builders constructed identical

houses and the same storm blasted each with merciless fury, but the builders themselves were completely different kinds of men. That means they built their houses according to entirely different standards. One chose to build on truth; the other built upon wishful thinking. The first builder is the type who does more than hear what Christ has to say. According to Jesus' own words, he hears and acts upon the truth. Interestingly, the second builder hears the very same things . . . but he stops there. He deliberately does not act upon what he hears. Jesus called the first builder "wise" and the second builder "foolish." Curiously, no one can tell by looking at the builders which one hears and acts and which one merely hears. It takes a storm to reveal which is which.

Eventually, the difference between the two houses became obvious. One "did not fall" (v. 25); the other "fell—and great was its fall" (v. 27). The wise builder had so constructed his life that no amount of testing, no extent of difficulty, was sufficient to bring him down. Why? The story tells us it is because "it had been founded on the rock" (v. 25). It takes no great theologian to identify what the rock represents . . . Christ Himself. The wise builder turned to the Lord Jesus Christ in simple faith and, acting upon the truth he learned, built his life accordingly. This gave him a solid and secure foundation, unlike his counterpart, whose life was foolishly built on sand.

As I think through the story, two enduring principles emerge.

First, *if you are only hearing and reading the truth, you are not prepared for life's storms.* In this information era, it is easy for us to become fascinated by more and more words, interested in intriguing concepts—making the process of gathering data an end in itself rather than acting upon the truth that is presented. The foolish builder heard everything the wise builder heard. The only difference was his refusal to do something about it. Small wonder Jesus frequently punctuated His remarks with the reminder "He who has ears to hear, let him hear!" To listen with no plan to act—to read with no interest in responding—is to miss the whole point of Christ's great message.

Second, *if your foundation is sure, no storm will cause your life to collapse or cause you to lose hope.* The rains of adversity will fall, no question about it. That's life. The floods of misery and heartache will rise, for sure. No one can dodge such harsh realities. And the winds of pressure will howl, threatening both your security and your sanity. But your life will not collapse, and hope will endure!

Hope Even in Trials

Believers can have hope even when suffering, because we have a permanent inheritance—a secure home in heaven. And our place there is reserved under the safekeeping, under the constant, omnipotent surveillance of almighty God. Furthermore, He has guaranteed that we will receive our inheritance because we are "protected by the power of God through faith for a salvation ready to be revealed in the last time (1 Peter 1:5). No disorder, no disease, not even death itself can weaken or threaten God's ultimate protection over our lives. Our souls are divinely protected.

Suffering and trials are inevitable; as long as we live in a fallen world, where things don't work according to God's standard, we will face trials. However, nothing is beyond God's control. Nothing comes to us that didn't first pass through the fingers of God. And we have His promise that all things will be used for our ultimate good (Romans 8:28–39). Therefore, we have every reason to rejoice during our suffering.

In this you greatly rejoice, even though now for a little while, if necessary, you have been distressed by various trials, so that the proof of your faith, being more precious than gold which is perishable, even though tested by fire, may be found to result in praise and glory and honor at the revelation of Jesus Christ. (1 Peter 1:6–7)

These verses teach us three lessons about trials.

First, *trials are often necessary*, proving the genuineness of our faith and at the same time teaching us humility. Trials not only reveal our helplessness, but they also put us on our faces before God . . . where we should be, regardless.

Second, *trials are distressing*, teaching us compassion so that we never make light of another's test or cruelly force others to smile while enduring it. Having endured trials allows us to provide hope to another without becoming trite.

Third, *trials come in various forms*. This variety is like different temperature settings on God's furnace. The settings are adjusted to burn off our dross, to temper us or soften us according to what meets our highest need. It is in God's refining fire that the authenticity of our faith is revealed, not only to others but to us as well.

God's Approval for Us

The Bible is filled with reminders of God's care for us, His plan for our welfare, and what our relationship with Him should be. The psalmist writes of God with free-flowing delight:

Bless the LORD, O my soul;
And all that is within me, bless His
  holy name!
Bless the LORD, O my soul,
And forget not all His benefits:
Who forgives all your iniquities,
Who heals all your diseases,
Who redeems your life from
  destruction,
Who crowns you with lovingkindness
  and tender mercies,
Who satisfies your mouth with good
  things,
So that your youth is renewed like the
  eagle's. . . .

For as the heavens are high above the
    earth,
So great is His mercy toward those
    who fear Him;
As far as the east is from the west,
So far has He removed our
    transgressions from us.
As a father pities his children,
So the LORD pities those who fear
    Him.
For He knows our frame;
He remembers that we are dust.
    (Psalm 103:1–5, 11–14 NKJV)

What a relief! God understands our
limits, and He realizes our struggles.
He knows how much pressure we can
take. He knows what measure of grace
and mercy and strength we'll require.

He knows how we're put together. Furthermore, He orchestrates all things to become the means of our experiencing His best.

> "For I know the plans that I have for you," declares the LORD, "plans for welfare and not for calamity to give you a future and a hope. Then you will call upon Me and come and pray to Me, and I will listen to you." (Jeremiah 29:11–12)

Isn't that wonderful? "I have plans for you, My son, My daughter," God says. "And they are great plans." Plans for your welfare and not your calamity. Plans to give you a future and a hope. It is God's agenda that His people never lose hope. Each new dawn it is as if He smiles from heaven, saying, "Hope again . . . hope again!"

Contrary to public opinion, God doesn't sit in heaven with His jaws clenched, His arms folded in disapproval, and a deep frown on His brow. He is not ticked off at His children for all the times we trip over our feet and fall flat. He is a loving Father, and we are precious in His sight, the delight of His heart. After all, He "has qualified us to share in the inheritance of the saints in Light" (Colossians 1:12).

Think of it! God has put us in His inheritance! Remember that the next time you think God is coming down on you. You have reason to give thanks. You don't have to qualify yourself for His kingdom.

His grace has rescued you. He has already qualified you by accomplishing a great deliverance in your life.

> For He rescued us from the domain of darkness, and transferred us to the kingdom of His beloved Son, in whom we have redemption, the forgiveness of sins. (Colossians 1:13–14)

Sometimes it's encouraging to thumb through the Scriptures and read promises that tell us what God thinks of us, especially in a world where people are continually telling us all the things they have against us and all the things they see wrong with us. God is not only "for us," according to Romans 8:31, but He is constantly giving great gifts to us.

Every good thing given and every perfect gift is from above, coming down from the Father of lights, with whom there is no variation or shifting shadow. (James 1:17)

In other words, there is no alteration or modification in God's giving, regardless of how we may turn away. No shifting shadow on our part causes Him to become moody and hold back His gifts to us. When we lose hope, it's difficult to rest in that truth. When we lose hope, we first begin to wonder if somehow God has ceased to care or has decided to punish us without revealing the reason. So let me make it simple.

God is for us.

Make it personal. Say, "God is for me."

Remember that tomorrow morning when you don't feel like He is. Remember that when you have failed. Remember that when you have sinned and guilt slams you to the mat.

"God is for me."

Let me encourage you to say it out loud. You need to hear those words. Repeat them over and over until you believe them.

God's Estimation of Us

Let me ask you a question. It will be especially difficult to answer if you've lost hope, but do your best to answer honestly, even if your family or friends might find it shocking. Ready? Here it is:

Do you believe that God thinks you are valuable?

And coming to Him as to a living stone which has been rejected by men, but is choice and precious in the sight of God, you also, as living stones, are being built up as a spiritual house for a holy priesthood, to offer up spiritual sacrifices acceptable to God through Jesus Christ. For this is contained in Scripture:

"Behold, I lay in Zion a choice stone,
a precious corner stone,
    And he who believes in Him will
not be disappointed."

(1 Peter 2:4–6)

The metaphor woven through this passage is that of a building. Christ is the cornerstone, and His children are living stones that make up the building. Each time someone trusts Christ as Savior, another stone is quarried out of the pit of sin and fitted into the spiritual house He's building through the work of the Holy Spirit. And carefully overseeing the construction is Christ, who is the hands-on contractor of this eternal edifice.

Each of us is His living stone. God is the Master Architect, and every stone is being placed exactly where He designed it to fit. Furthermore, as any experienced stone mason will confirm, there are no unimportant stones. Because you have been chosen to become a part of His house, you can be certain God finds you immensely valuable. Never forget that, even on those blue days. We are living stones in a spiritual house.

We Are Chosen by God

Why did God choose us? Not because we did anything that impressed Him. It wasn't the size of our faith or the greatness of our intellect. It certainly wasn't because we first chose Him. It was entirely by grace. Grace prompted by love.

The Lord chooses us for reasons only He can answer. He is sovereign, and He can give grace to whomever He pleases. He sets His love upon us because, out of the goodness and grace of His own heart, He declares, "I want you to be Mine."

Isn't that humbling? Jesus said to His disciples,

You did not choose Me but I chose you, and appointed you that you would go and bear fruit, and that your fruit would remain, so that whatever you ask of the Father in My name He may give to you (John 15:16).

In other words, we didn't hunt Him down; He hunted us down. We didn't work half our lives to find Him; He gave His life to find us. Being chosen by God says a lot more about Him than it does about us!

We Are God's Own Possession

Nevertheless, think of the value of being owned by God. What incredible worth that bestows on us, what inexplicable dignity! We are "A PEOPLE FOR GOD'S OWN POSSESSION" (1 Peter 2:9). And the price paid for us was unimaginably high—the blood of Jesus Christ. That's how we belong to Him. That's enough to bring a smile to anyone's face. But there is more.

We are a people who have received mercy.

> For you once were not a people, but now you are the people of God; you had not received mercy, but now you have received mercy. (1 Peter 2:10)

As a result of God's mercy, we have become a people who are uniquely and exclusively cared for by God. The fact that we are recipients of His mercy makes all the difference in the world as to how we respond to difficult times. He watches over us with enormous interest.

Why? Because of His immense mercy, freely demonstrated in spite of our not deserving it. What guilt-relieving, encouraging news!

God Is for Us

Romans 8:31 says, "God is for us." In devoted love, He chose us. In great grace, He stooped to accept us into His family. In immense mercy, He still finds us wandering, forgives our foolish ways, and frees us to serve Him even though we don't deserve such treatment.

With God on our side like this, how can we lose? If God did hesitate to put everything on the line for us, embracing our condition and exposing Himself to the worst by sending His own Son, is there anything else He wouldn't gladly and freely do for us? The One who died for us—who was raised to life for us!—is in the presence of God at this very moment, advocating for us. Do you think anyone could drive a wedge between us and Christ's love for us?

I am absolutely convinced that nothing—nothing living or dead, angelic or demonic, today or tomorrow, high or low, thinkable or unthinkable—absolutely nothing can get between us and God's love because of the way that Jesus our Master has embraced us.

His Suffering, Our Hope

For Christ also died for sins once for all, the just for the unjust, so that He might bring us to God, having been put to death in the flesh, but made alive in the spirit. (1 Peter 3:18)

Why did Christ die? "So that He might bring us to God." Our Lord Jesus Christ, in dying on the cross, provided us with access into heaven. As a result of His death, the access to heaven is now permanently paved. It is available to all who believe in the Lord Jesus Christ.

He was "put to death in the flesh, but made alive in the spirit." So what is He doing now? He is "at the right hand of God" (1 Peter 3:22).

Maybe you did not know that—a lot of people don't know what Christ is currently doing. He has ascended from this earth, and He has gone back to the place of glory in bodily form. At this moment, Christ is sitting at the right hand of God, making intercession for us. He is moved by our needs. He is touched with the feelings of our infirmities. He is there for us, His people, and He is interceding for us. Since He is at the right hand of God, there is no question of His place of authority.

Hope Begins with a Relationship with God

During His earthly ministry, Jesus was the perfect model of a person enjoying intimate fellowship with our heavenly Father and a close walk with Him. However, His example reveals how imperfect we are. Unlike Jesus, we are separated from God by sin, and we are powerless to restore this relationship on our own. We can never match the example of Jesus. However, we can enjoy intimate fellowship with God through His Son.

If you want to have a relationship with God, you need to understand four vital truths. Let's look at each marker in detail.

Our Spiritual Condition: Totally Depraved
The first truth is rather personal. One look in the mirror of Scripture, and our human condition becomes painfully clear:

There is none righteous, not even one;
There is none who understands,
There is none who seeks for God;
All have turned aside, together they
   have become useless;

There is none who does good,
There is not even one.

(Romans 3:10–12)

We are all sinners through and through—totally depraved. Now, that doesn't mean we've committed every atrocity known to humankind. We're not as *bad* as we can be, just as *bad off* as we can be. Sin colors all our thoughts, motives, words, and actions.

You still don't believe it? Look around. Everything around us bears the smudge marks of our sinful nature. Despite our best effort to create a perfect world, crime statistics continue to soar, divorce rates keep climbing, and families keep crumbling.

Something has gone terribly wrong in our society and in ourselves, something deadly. Contrary to how the world would repackage it, "me-first" living doesn't equal rugged individuality and freedom; it equals death. As Paul said in his letter to the Romans, "The wages of sin is death" (6:23)—our spiritual and physical death that comes from God's righteous judgment of our sin, along with all the emotional and practical effects of the separation we experience on a daily basis.

God's Character: Infinitely Holy

How can God judge each of us for a sinful state we were born into? Our total depravity is only half the answer. The other half is God's infinite holiness.

The fact that we know things are not as they should be points us to a standard of goodness beyond ourselves. Our sense of injustice in life on this side of eternity implies a perfect standard of justice beyond our reality. That standard and source is God Himself. And God's standard of holiness contrasts starkly with our sinful condition.

Scripture says, "God is Light, and in Him there is no darkness at all" (1 John 1:5). He is absolutely holy—which creates a problem for us. If He's so pure, how can we who are so impure relate to Him?

Perhaps we could try to be better people, try to tilt the balance in favor of our good deeds, or seek out methods for self-improvement. Throughout history, people have attempted to live up to God's standard by keeping the Ten Commandments or living by their own code of ethics. Unfortunately, no one can come close to satisfying the demands of God's law. Romans 3:20 says, "For no one can ever be made right with God by doing what the law commands. The law simply shows us how sinful we are" (Romans 3:20 NLT).

Our Need: A Substitute

So here we are, sinners by nature and sinners by choice, trying to pull ourselves up by our own bootstraps to attain a relationship with our holy Creator. But every time we try, we fall flat on our faces. We can't live a good enough life to make up for our sin, because God's standard isn't "good enough"—it's perfection. And we can't make amends for the offense our sin has created without dying for it.

Who can get us out of this mess?

If someone could live perfectly, honoring God's law, and could bear sin's death penalty for us—in our place—then we would be saved from our predicament. But is there such a person? Thankfully, yes!

Meet your substitute—Jesus Christ. He is the One who suffered the punishment of death you deserve!

> [God] made Him who knew no sin to be sin on our behalf, so that we might become the righteousness of God in Him. (2 Corinthians 5:21)

God's Provision: A Savior

God rescued us by sending His Son, Jesus, to die for our sin on the cross (1 John 4:9–10). Jesus was fully human and fully God (John 1:1, 18), a truth that ensures

His understanding of our weakness, His power to forgive, and His ability to bridge the gap between God and us (Romans 5:6–11). In short, we are "justified as a gift by His grace through the redemption which is in Christ Jesus" (Romans 3:24). Two words in this verse warrant further explanation: *justified* and *redemption*.

Justification is God's act of mercy in which He declares believing sinners righteous, while they are still in their sinning state. Justification doesn't mean God *makes* us righteous so that we never sin again; rather, He *declares* us righteous—much like a judge pardons a guilty criminal. Because Jesus took our sin upon Himself and suffered our judgment on the cross, God forgives our debt and proclaims us pardoned.

Redemption is God's act of paying the ransom price to release us from our bondage of sin. Held hostage by Satan, we were shackled by the iron chains of sin and death. Like a loving parent whose child has been kidnapped, God willingly paid the ransom for you. And what a price He paid! He gave His only Son to bear our sins—past, present, and future. Jesus' death and resurrection broke our chains and set us free to become children of God (Romans 6:16–18, 22; Galatians 4:4–7).

Placing Your Faith in Christ

These four truths describe how God has provided a way to Himself through His Son, Jesus Christ. Because the price has been paid in full by God, we must respond to His free gift of eternal life in total faith and confidence in Him to save us. We must step forward into the relationship with God that He has prepared for us-not by doing good works or being a good person, but by coming to Him just as we are and accepting His justification and redemption by faith.

For by grace you have been saved through faith; and that not of yourselves, it is the gift of God; not as a result of works, so that no one may boast. (Ephesians 2:8–9)

We accept God's gift of salvation simply by placing our faith in Christ alone for the forgiveness of our sins.

Would you like to enter a relationship

with your Creator by trusting Christ as your Savior? If so, here's a simple prayer you can use to express your faith:

Dear God,

I know my sin has put a barrier between You and me. Thank You for sending Your Son, Jesus, to die in my place. I trust in Jesus alone to forgive my sins, and I accept His gift of eternal life. I ask Jesus to be my personal Savior and the Lord of my life. Thank You.

In Jesus' name, amen.

No other decision you will ever make can compare with the one that puts you in a right relationship with God through His Son, Jesus Christ, who loved us and gave Himself for us!

Hope for Life

Once you have placed your trust in Jesus Christ to save you from the penalty of your sin, you never again have to worry about condemnation—not from other people and not even from God (Romans 8:1). Guilt and shame have no place in the life of a believer; however, we are still prone to sin. We will fail in our efforts to live a life that honors God, and we inevitably harm others by the poor choices we make and the sinful acts we commit. Because Jesus paid the penalty for our sin, we will never suffer the eternal consequences for our wrongdoing. However, unresolved sin can complicate our lives with earthly consequences, frustrate the Lord's desire to bless us, and cause others great heartache. Despite our secure relationship with God, sin is still a deadly serious matter.

Fortunately, the Lord has given us a means by which we can clear away the clutter of wrongdoing. If you have unresolved sin in your life, consider taking the following steps, which give practical application to principles taught in Scripture.

Stop. Accept the truth of your poor choices or outright sin and own the responsibility for the damage your action or inaction has caused.

Confess. Confess your failure to the Lord in prayer and commit yourself to turning from it. Ask Him for His help. He has promised to provide you with the strength to meet this challenge (1 Corinthians 10:13). If your sin has harmed another person, go to him or her and admit how you have failed or have contributed to making a situation worse. Be careful not to include any mention of his or her wrongdoing (even if it is greater than your own), and resist the temptation to minimize yours.

Restore. Apologize, showing genuine concern for how you have hurt the other person and damaged your relationship. Your authentic sorrow should reflect the intensity of his or her pain.

Rest. Receive the Lord's forgiveness and accept that the other person may or may not respond as you might desire.

Forgiveness is not something you deserve or have the right to demand. His or her choice to forgive must be made freely.

Review. Without being too hard on yourself, try to discover why you chose to act as you did. Choices arise from expectations—usually unconscious ones. Ask the Lord to show you what you don't see so that you can replace destructive coping with constructive choosing (Psalm 139:23–24). Then ask Him to cleanse your heart of any desire for sin (Psalm 51:10).

This is not a magic formula. It is not something you must do to please God or to earn His favor. Because Christ died for your sin and rose from the dead to give you life, your heavenly Father will always be pleased with you. These steps are merely a means by which you can keep your life free from the distractions and hindrances of unresolved sin. The Lord has blessings in store that exceed your wildest imaginings. Don't let anything come between you!

Hope for Eternity

Will there be suffering as we do battle with the enemy—Satan, sin, and the world? Certainly. Will it be painful? Without a doubt. But after the dust settles, our Commander-in-Chief will pin medals of honor on our lapels.

And, after you have suffered for a little while, the God of all grace who called you to his eternal glory in Christ will himself restore, confirm, strengthen, and establish you. (1 Peter 5:10 NET)

Talk about hope for eternity! Here is the biblical portrait of a well-grounded, stable, mature Christian. Christ will make sure the portrait of our lives looks like that, for He Himself will hold the brush. And His hand is vastly more powerful than anyone else's.

When you doubt yourself and begin to lose hope, place your confidence in Christ and experience the Rising Hope.

Ordinary People, Great Lives

ISBN 978-0-8499-1382-2

ISBN 978-0-8499-1386-0

ISBN 978-0-8499-1383-9

ISBN 978-0-8499-1342-6

Available Now

INSIGHT FOR LIVING

THOMAS NELSON
Since 1798

For other products and live events,
visit us at: thomasnelson.com

Ordinary People, Great Lives

ISBN 978-0-8499-1385-3

ISBN 978-0-8499-1749-3

ISBN 978-0-8499-0190-4

ISBN 978-0-8499-1389-1

Available Now

INSIGHT FOR LIVING

THOMAS NELSON
Since 1798

For other products and live events,
visit us at: thomasnelson.com

Draw closer to the Gospel of
Jesus Christ with these additional titles.

ISBN 978-1-4002-0247-8

In *Walk with Jesus*, a forty day lent devotional, readers go on a compelling journey through the life and ministry of Jesus.

Mission Possible is the adaptation of *Walk with Jesus* which helps elementary school age children understand the truth about Jesus Christ.

ISBN 978-1-4003-1443-0

INSIGHT FOR LIVING

THOMAS NELSON
Since 1798

For other products and live events,
visit us at: **thomasnelson.com**